The Illustrated

Student
COOKBOOK

a step-by-step guide for everyday essentials

Keda Black

Photography by Deirdre Rooney   Illustrations by Alice Chadwick

MURDOCH BOOKS

Contents

Foreword

With little time, little money and limited kitchen equipment, the gourmet life of a student is too often a boring story of toast and unhealthy takeaways. There are so many other things to plan and think about when you are at university...

With this book, you need worry no more. If you keep a limited but wise selection of foods in the cupboard and fridge, and stop by the greengrocer's from time to time, you'll have just about everything you need to make up some interesting, filling and healthy meals in no time.

What's that you say? « *But I can't even boil an egg!* » Just you wait and see: we'll show you how to make up something as basic as a sandwich, or how to cook an omelette. And for those who already have a few skills, this book has plenty of ideas to vary meals — whether using the stovetop, a mini-oven or, of course, a microwave. And some recipes require no cooking at all! Whether you're craving a *sweet* treat, WARM COMFORT FOOD, or a *filling breakfast* to start a big day, we have something for you, **meat-eaters**, *vegoes*, **FOOD JUNKIES**...

Every recipe has a photo to tempt you **and** illustrated « step-by-step » instructions to guide you through. You're going to love it!

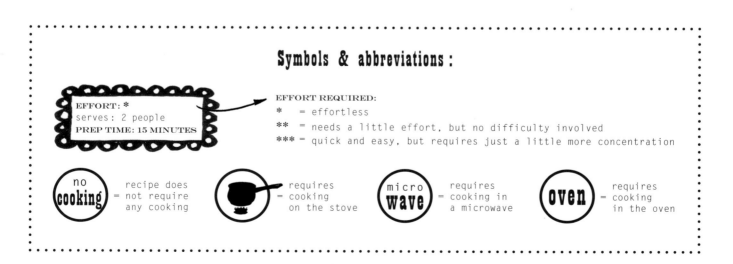

Symbols & abbreviations :

EFFORT: *
serves: 2 people
PREP TIME: 15 MINUTES

EFFORT REQUIRED:
* = effortless
** = needs a little effort, but no difficulty involved
*** = quick and easy, but requires just a little more concentration

no cooking recipe does = not require any cooking

requires = cooking on the stove

micro wave requires = cooking in a microwave

oven requires = cooking in the oven

Mozzarella, Tomato and more

EFFORT: *
serves: 2 people
PREP TIME: 15 MINUTES

no cooking

INGREDIENTS:

2 small ripe tomatoes
+
1 lemon
+
1 ripe avocado*
*OR 3-4 ripe fresh figs + 1 teaspoon clear honey

OLIVE OIL

salt
& black pepper

MOZZARELLA
2 balls of mozzarella*

good crusty bread

a few sprigs of fresh basil

*(buffalo mozzarella is a bit more expensive, but far more tasty)

EQUIPMENT:

knife

chopping board

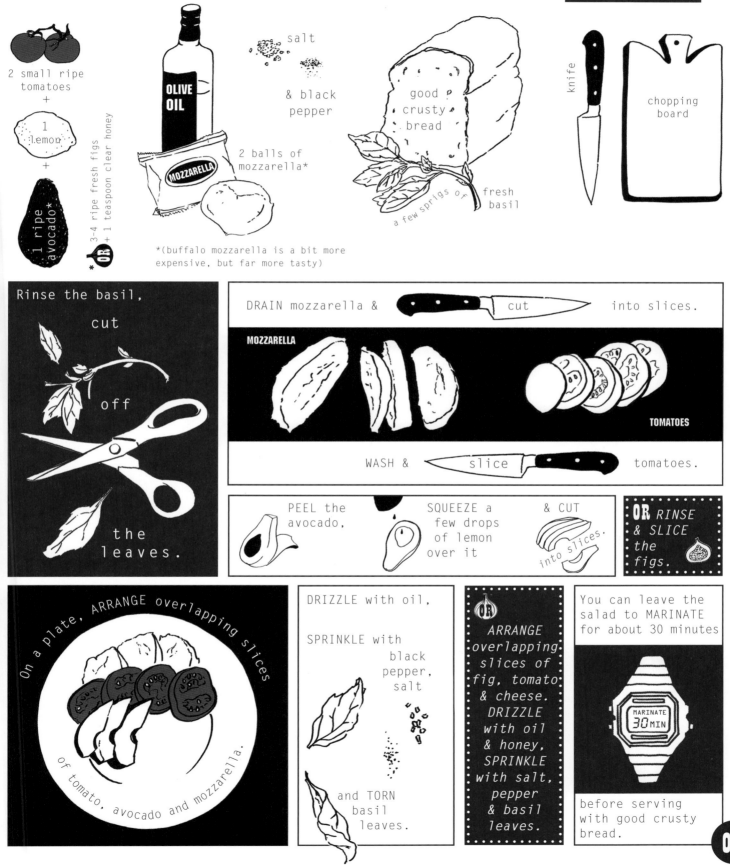

Rinse the basil, cut off the leaves.

DRAIN mozzarella & cut into slices.

MOZZARELLA

TOMATOES

WASH & slice tomatoes.

PEEL the avocado, SQUEEZE a few drops of lemon over it & CUT into slices.

OR RINSE & SLICE the figs.

On a plate, ARRANGE overlapping slices of tomato, avocado and mozzarella.

DRIZZLE with oil, SPRINKLE with black pepper, salt and TORN basil leaves.

OR ARRANGE overlapping slices of fig, tomato & cheese. DRIZZLE with oil & honey, SPRINKLE with salt, pepper & basil leaves.

You can leave the salad to MARINATE for about 30 minutes

MARINATE 30 MIN

before serving with good crusty bread.

salad days

01

Real Tabouleh

EFFORT: **
serves: 2 people
PREP TIME: 30 MINUTES

no cooking

INGREDIENTS:

tbs = tablespoon

1 handful **BULGHUR WHEAT** (about 40 g / 1½ oz / ¼ cup)

2 spring onions or 1 shallot

1 bunch of flat-leaf parsley

1 bunch of mint

OLIVE OIL 1-2 tbs

salt + pepper

SA[LT]

1 lemon

EQUIPMENT:

chopping knife board

saucepan *or kettle*

Optional:

a ripe tomato

a small chunk of cucumber

a small piece of red capsicum (pepper)

if in season, half a peach or 1 plum (ripe).

PLACE bulghur wheat in a bowl and cover with boiling water (about 200 ml / 6 fl oz / ¾ cup, or a **LARGE** glass).

salt

about 200 ml

Cover with

a *plate*

&

LEAVE ASIDE.

RINSE the herbs, PAT DRY between sheets of kitchen paper. DETACH leaves from stems. CHOP leaves finely. Discard stems.

CHOP finely.

PEEL & CHOP the onions finely. If using, CHOP the cucmber, tomato and / or capsicum into very small dice...

...as well as the peach or plum, if using.

After about 30 mins, DRAIN the bulghur wheat if necessary (it may not have absorbed all the water).

PUT it into a bowl. ADD:

the herbs

lemon juice

oil

& the vegetables

&

some pepper.

MIX *gently* with a fork.

TASTE & ADJUST the seasonings if necessary (oil, lemon, pepper & salt).

This tabouleh will be very green and not too filling. Eat as a salad or try with foil-baked fish for instance. It's ideal for a picnic or a packed lunch, along with some fresh cheese and a chunk of bread.

salad days

02

Super Salad
Chicken, Chickpeas & Bulghur Wheat

EFFORT: **
serves : 2 people
PREP TIME: 30 MINUTES

INGREDIENTS :

tbs = tablespoon
tsp = teaspoon

1 small tin of CHICK PEAS

1 handful BULGHUR WHEAT (about 40 g / 2 oz / ¼ cup)

1 chicken breast

a good pinch of CUMIN seeds

1 lemon

6 sprigs of fresh coriander

pepper

salt

1 spring onion (or 1 small shallot)

OLIVE OIL 4 tbs (¼ cup)

EQUIPMENT :

chopping knife board

frying pan

saucepan *or kettle

PLACE bulghur wheat into a bowl with a little salt

water

POUR in about 200 ml (6 fl oz / ¾ cup) boiling water.

COVER with a plate... **&**

LEAVE ASIDE.

DRAIN the chickpeas.

*it should be cooked through, check by cutting in half.

HEAT up 1 tbs olive oil. ADD the chicken & cumin.

cumin oil chicken

SEAR both sides

ADD a glass of water.

LOWER the heat *slightly* & SIMMER for about 15 minutes.

Cooking time depends on the thickness of the meat*.

Put onto a PLATE & CUT into small pieces.

MAKE a vinaigrette DRESSING in a screw-top jar:

3 tbs olive oil

shake

salt pepper

2–3 tsp lemon juice

RINSE the coriander, pat DRY *gently*.

CHOP the onion.

& CHOP *finely*.

In a large bowl, COMBINE drained wheat, chickpeas, chopped onion, chicken pieces (along with cumin seeds) & vinaigrette.

sprinkle the coriander

MIX *very gently*.

>>> This salad is quite filling and makes for a light meal by itself!

salad days

03

Interesting Grated Carrots

EFFORT: **
serves: 2 people
PREP TIME: 20 MINUTES

no cooking

INGREDIENTS :

4 carrots
(preferably organic)

1 lemon

salt & pepper

OLIVE OIL
1-2 tablespoons
(about ⅛ cup)

EQUIPMENT:

simple grater

knife & chopping board

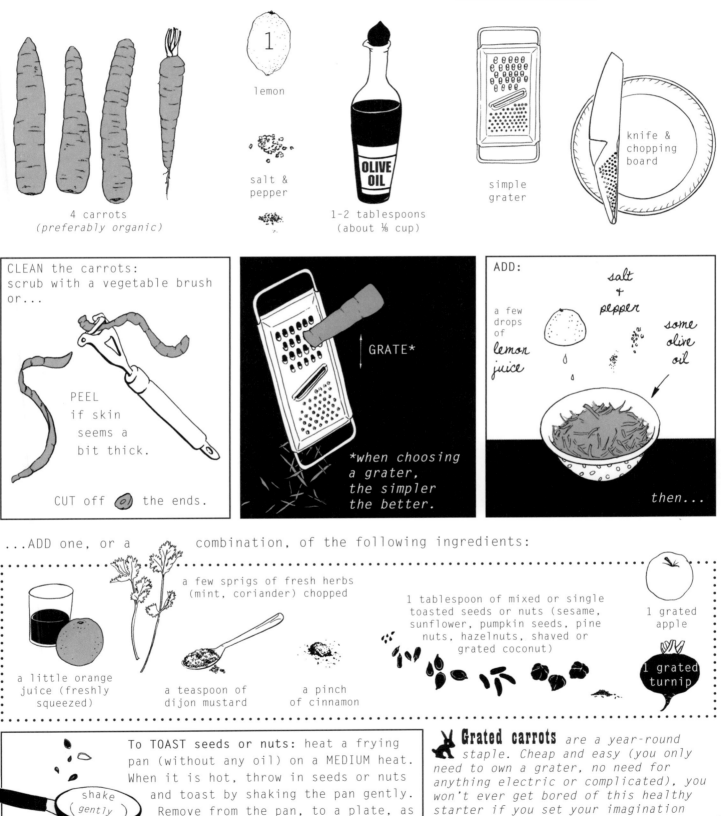

CLEAN the carrots: scrub with a vegetable brush or...

PEEL if skin seems a bit thick.

CUT off ⬭ the ends.

GRATE*

*when choosing a grater, the simpler the better.

ADD:

a few drops of *lemon juice*

salt + pepper

some olive oil

then...

...ADD one, or a combination, of the following ingredients:

a little orange juice (freshly squeezed)

a few sprigs of fresh herbs (mint, coriander) chopped

a teaspoon of dijon mustard

a pinch of cinnamon

1 tablespoon of mixed or single toasted seeds or nuts (sesame, sunflower, pumpkin seeds, pine nuts, hazelnuts, shaved or grated coconut)

1 grated apple

1 grated turnip

To TOAST seeds or nuts: heat a frying pan (without any oil) on a MEDIUM heat. When it is hot, throw in seeds or nuts and toast by shaking the pan gently. Remove from the pan, to a plate, as soon as they start to brown lightly.

shake (*gently*)

Grated carrots *are a year-round staple. Cheap and easy (you only need to own a grater, no need for anything electric or complicated), you won't ever get bored of this healthy starter if you set your imagination free, or simply go along with the few ideas above.*

salad days

04

Crumpet Toasties

EFFORT: **
serves: 2 people
PREP TIME: 15 MINUTES

oven *or* micro wave
with grill option *with grill option*

INGREDIENTS :

2 slices of prosciutto or plain leg ham

black pepper

4 - 6 crumpets

1 apple

about 100 g (4 oz) cheese

EQUIPMENT :

knife

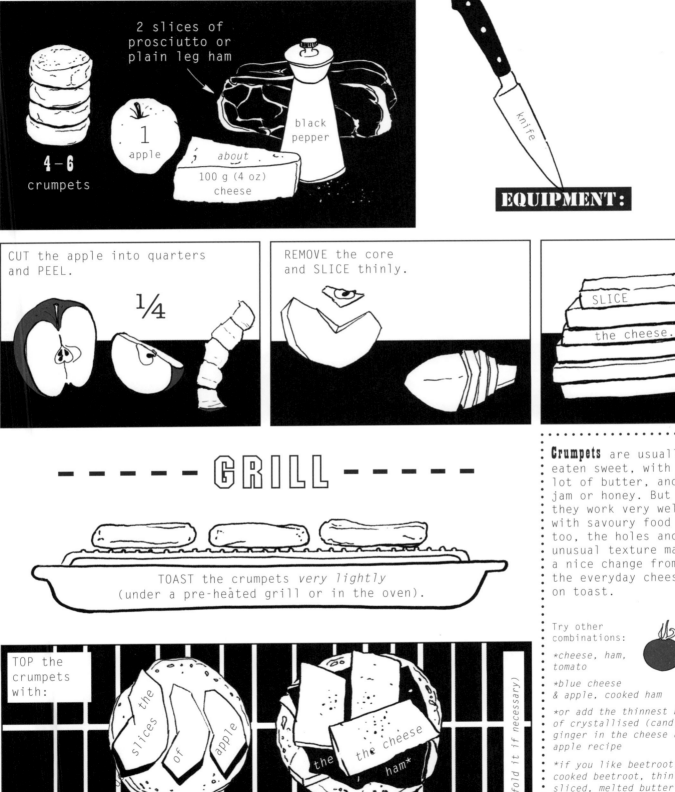

CUT the apple into quarters and PEEL.

¼

REMOVE the core and SLICE thinly.

SLICE the cheese.

- - - - GRILL - - - - -

TOAST the crumpets *very lightly*
(under a pre-heated grill or in the oven).

TOP the crumpets with:

the slices of apple

the ham*

the the cheese

*(fold it if necessary)

Add some black pepper and TOAST until the cheese melts and turns golden.

Crumpets are usually eaten sweet, with a lot of butter, and jam or honey. But they work very well with savoury food too, the holes and unusual texture making a nice change from the everyday cheese on toast.

Try other combinations:

*cheese, ham, tomato

*blue cheese & apple, cooked ham

*or add the thinnest bit of crystallised (candied) ginger in the cheese and apple recipe

*if you like beetroot: cooked beetroot, thinly sliced, melted butter and cheddar, black pepper etc....

quick fix

05

How to cook an Omelette

EFFORT: ***
serves: 2 people
PREP TIME: 10 MINUTES

INGREDIENTS :

tsp = teaspoon

6
eggs

pepper & salt

20 g (²/₃ oz/ 4 tsp) *butter*

EQUIPMENT :

frying pan *small or medium**

spatula
or wooden spoon
or large wooden fork
(or silicone)

*If the pan is too big, the egg mixture will spread out too thinly and the omelette will be dry. If it is too small, the omelette will be a bit too thick, but this is a lesser evil as you will simply have to cook the omelette a little longer on a lower heat, at the risk of making it a bit too dry on the outside. A good omelette must remain quite moist.

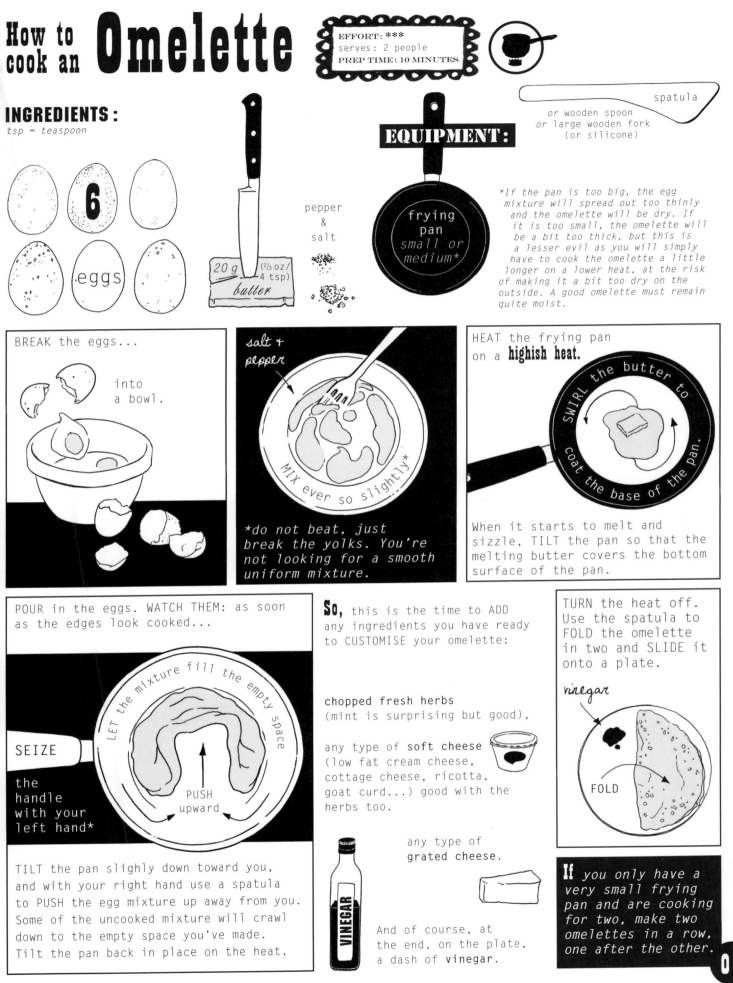

BREAK the eggs...
into a bowl.

salt + pepper

MIX ever so slightly*

*do not beat, just break the yolks. You're not looking for a smooth uniform mixture.

HEAT the frying pan on a **highish heat.**

SWIRL the butter to coat the base of the pan.

When it starts to melt and sizzle, TILT the pan so that the melting butter covers the bottom surface of the pan.

POUR in the eggs. WATCH THEM: as soon as the edges look cooked...

LET the mixture fill the empty space

SEIZE

the handle with your left hand*

PUSH upward

TILT the pan slighly down toward you, and with your right hand use a spatula to PUSH the egg mixture up away from you. Some of the uncooked mixture will crawl down to the empty space you've made. Tilt the pan back in place on the heat.

So, this is the time to ADD any ingredients you have ready to CUSTOMISE your omelette:

chopped fresh herbs (mint is surprising but good),

any type of **soft cheese** (low fat cream cheese, cottage cheese, ricotta, goat curd...) good with the herbs too.

any type of **grated cheese.**

VINEGAR

And of course, at the end, on the plate, a dash of **vinegar.**

TURN the heat off. Use the spatula to FOLD the omelette in two and SLIDE it onto a plate.

vinegar

FOLD

If *you only have a very small frying pan and are cooking for two, make two omelettes in a row, one after the other.*

quick fix

06

Potato Gratin in the microwave

EFFORT: **
serves: 2 people#
PREP TIME: 40 MINUTES

micro **wave** or oven

#with leftovers for the next day

INGREDIENTS :

about 5 0 0 g (1 lb) potatoes

1 clove of garlic

salt + pepper

a knob of butter

double cream 300 ml **or** a mix of cream & milk

(10 fl oz/1¼ cups)

EQUIPMENT:

rectangular plastic box*
(microwavable)

or

rectangular or oval gratin dish*
(ovenproof)

and

knife

*about 30 cm (12 inches) long

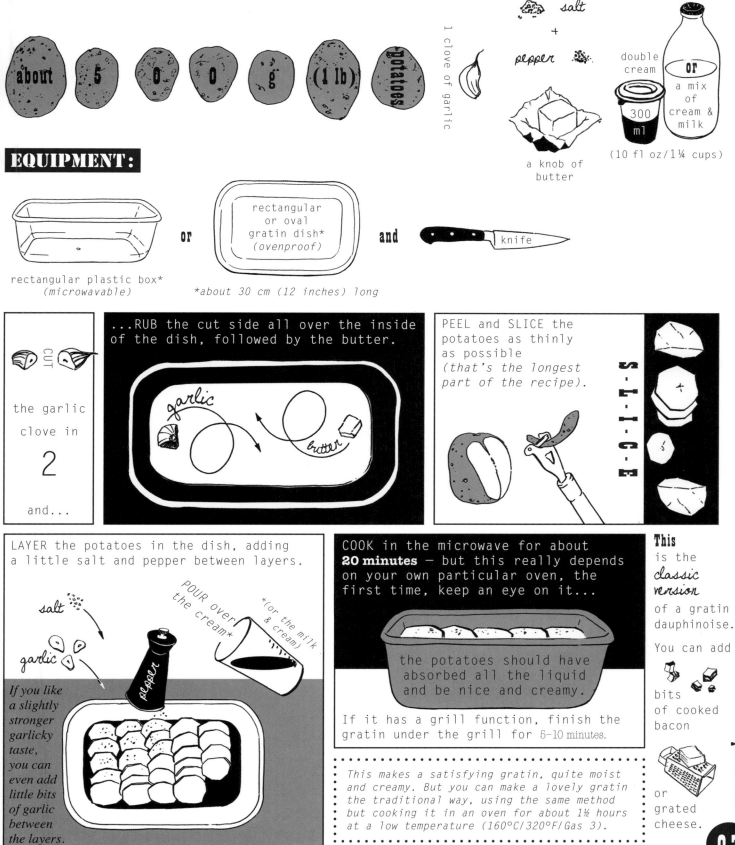

CUT the garlic clove in 2 and...

...RUB the cut side all over the inside of the dish, followed by the butter.

garlic   butter

PEEL and SLICE the potatoes as thinly as possible *(that's the longest part of the recipe).*

S-L-I-C-E

LAYER the potatoes in the dish, adding a little salt and pepper between layers.

salt
garlic
POUR over the cream*
*(or the milk & cream)

If you like a slightly stronger garlicky taste, you can even add little bits of garlic between the layers.

COOK in the microwave for about **20 minutes** — but this really depends on your own particular oven, the first time, keep an eye on it...

the potatoes should have absorbed all the liquid and be nice and creamy.

If it has a grill function, finish the gratin under the grill for 5-10 minutes.

This makes a satisfying gratin, quite moist and creamy. But you can make a lovely gratin the traditional way, using the same method but cooking it in an oven for about 1½ hours at a low temperature (160°C/320°F/Gas 3).

This is the *classic version* of a gratin dauphinoise.

You can add bits of cooked bacon or grated cheese.

quick fix

07

Baked Potatoes
healthy & quick

EFFORT: *
serves: 2 people
PREP TIME: 15 MINUTES

micro **wave**
or oven

INGREDIENTS:

2 LARGE potatoes

pepper & salt

INDIAN PICKLE

cottage CHEESE

cheddar*
*grated

toppings

butter

EQUIPMENT:

grater

OR FOR THE OVEN:

metal knives *or* skewers

FOR THE MICROWAVE:

plastic box*

with a lid

*big enough for the potatoes

OR

ALUMINIUM FOIL

MICROWAVE:

WASH the potatoes *thoroughly* BUT do not dry!

PIERCE holes all over *with a knife*

pointed

PLACE in the microwave and COOK for about 7-8 minutes.

*Potatoes should be tender when pierced with a knife but not completely soft.**

*You might need to adjust the cooking time according to the size of the potatoes and to your oven.

WRAP the potatoes in foil or place in a plastic container with a lid and LEAVE for 5 minutes outside the oven: this will finish the cooking.

5 min

OR

5 min

OVEN: *They will take at least an hour* at 200°C/400°F/Gas 6, *depending on the size of the potatoes.*

Pierce them with a metal skewer or knife, which you should leave in for cooking (*it will conduct the heat inside and speed up the process a little*).

attention!

DO NOT USE PLASTIC, or WOOD!

Then once the potatoes are ready:

SLIT the skin & add the TOPPINGS...

Salted butter & black pepper is great.

Grated cheese is delicious.

pickle

OR TRY cottage cheese + Indian Brinjal (aubergine) pickle.

Midnight Spaghetti

EFFORT: **
serves : 2 people
PREP TIME: 20 MINUTES

INGREDIENTS :

tbs = tablespoon

3 cloves of garlic

a good pinch
of dried chillies
(optional)

SPAGHETTI
200 g
(7 oz)

black pepper

& salt

4 tbs
(¼ cup)

*olive oil ***

EQUIPMENT:

LARGE
saucepan
&
colander
or sieve

knife

TAKE OUT a **LARGE** pan and HEAT some water (<u>at least</u> 2 litres/70 fl oz/ 8 cups). When it reaches a rolling boil, ADD some...

SALT

2 *litres* of water

...then PLUNGE in the pasta.

When the water comes back to the boil, check the time or put a timer on.*

*Follow guidelines from the packaging.

While the pasta is cooking,

PEEL the garlic and SLICE as *thinly* as possible.

---

the cooked pasta

a little *liquid*

*taste it: it should still be firm (al dente) — or not, cook it to your liking!

When your pasta is ready*, DRAIN it, but try to keep a little of the cooking liquid aside in a bowl.

PUT the pan back on a medium heat and pour in the oil.

garlic

oil

chillies

ADD
the garlic and chillies and cook briefly until garlic just starts to turn golden.

REMOVE from heat, ADD the drained pasta and reserved liquid.

MIX with the « sauce ».

MIX gently

pasta night

09

A good recipe for when the fridge is empty. An all-time classic often called « **aglio olio** *» (garlic & oil).*

Creamy lemon butter Pasta

INGREDIENTS :

200G PASTA (7 oz)

50 g of butter (2 oz / ½ stick)

200 ml cream* (6 fl oz / ¾ cup) *(single or double)

salt + pepper

1 lemon* *preferrably unwaxed or organic

EQUIPMENT:

grater or zester

lemon juicer

LARGE saucepan & colander or sieve

small frying pan

☞ This recipe also works with fresh pasta, which needs only a few minutes cooking.

BOIL water for the pasta: you need at least 1 litre (35 fl oz/4 cups) per 100 g (3½ oz) pasta. When it comes to a rolling boil, ADD the pasta and COOK for the required time.

pasta   salt

Rolling boil

← medium heat

While the pasta is cooking, WASH the lemon and GRATE its zest* finely (use the fine side of a grater).

SQUEEZE the juice.

*The lemon zest gives an interesting taste but leave it out if you don't have a grater or if the skin of the lemon is too smooth to be grated.

DRAIN the cooked pasta.

HEAT the butter in the pan on a low heat. ADD:

the cream

half the lemon juice

the zest

2 min

ATTENTION! LOW HEAT

LET this sauce SIMMER for about **2 MINUTES**. Taste and ADD more lemon if necessary, some SALT & PEPPER.

PUT the pasta in with the sauce & MIX gently.

Serve & eat!

Carbonara

EFFORT: **
serves: 2 people
PREP TIME: 20 MINUTES

INGREDIENTS :

4 slices of bacon
or pancetta

2 eggs

200 g LONG PASTA **(7 oz)**

spaghetti, tagliatelle
or linguine

10 g (2 teaspoons)
of butter

salt & pepper

50 g (2 oz) of grated
parmesan or pecorino cheese

EQUIPMENT:

LARGE
saucepan
&
colander
or sieve

knife & board

large bowl

the bacon or pancetta into cubes or strips.

cut

HEAT the butter in the pan and FRY the bacon (or pancetta), STIRRING from time to time, until the pieces are lightly browned.*

MEDIUM HEAT

EMPTY onto a plate.

*Cook them longer if you like them crunchy.

PUT water to BOIL in the pan (at least 2 litres/ 70 fl oz/8 cups), with a little salt. When it reaches a **ROLLING** boil, ADD the pasta and COOK for the recommended time.

2 litres

Meanwhile, BREAK the eggs in a large bowl and MIX in the grated cheese.

Add the fried bacon.

DRAIN the pasta.

DRAIN a little earlier if you like your pasta firmer.

Tip pasta into a bowl and stir to COMBINE with the « egg-cheese-bacon » mixture. Add PEPPER.

Extras

1. There was no cream in the original recipe!

2. The egg mixture should never go on the stove. It will cook when it comes into contact with the hot pasta.

3. It's always best to buy cheese whole and grate it freshly at home. Buy parmesan shavings rather than the grated powder-like kind if you find it. But ready-grated will do!

Serve sprinkled

with parmesan

cheese.

Wholewheat **Pasta & Rocket**

EFFORT: *
serves: 2 people
PREP TIME: 15 MINUTES

INGREDIENTS :

tbs = tablespoon
tsp = teaspoon

100 g (3½ oz)
1 bag of **ROCKET**

3 tbs
OLIVE OIL
(¼ cup)

TABASCO
or any form of chilli

salt

200 g of WHOLEWHEAT SPAGHETTI (7 oz)
(or other pasta shapes)

40 g (1½ oz) of parmesan
(preferrably grated from a whole piece)

EQUIPMENT:

LARGE
saucepan & colander or sieve

grater or peeler

COOK the pasta in a large quantity of salted boiling water (<u>at least</u> 2 litres/70 fl oz/8 cups) for the recommended time.

SALT

For 200 g of pasta you need at least **2 litres** of water

...so it's better to use a **LARGE** saucepan.

GRATE the parmesan...

or

SHAVE with a peeler.

DRAIN the pasta (retaining a little of the cooking liquid).

cooked pasta

a little *liquid*

RETURN the pasta to the pan.

Add:

the chilli

the liquid

the rocket

most of the parmesan

the oil

MIX gently...

& serve sprinkled with the remaining parmesan.

Extras

1. You can make this with fresh baby spinach leaves (also available in a bag). The leaves will « cook » in the still hot pasta.

2. You can also vary the cheeses — use something fresh, like ricotta, for example.

pasta night

12

SPRINKLE with peanuts
and torn mint
leaves

DIY Noodles

EFFORT: **
serves: 2 people
PREP TIME: 20 MINUTES

INGREDIENTS :

tbs = tablespoon
tsp = teaspoon

1 chicken breast

1 clove of garlic

and/or a piece of ginger

125 g (4 oz) of Asian Noodles*

*not thin rice noodles

OIL 4 tbs (¼ cup)

2 tbs SOY SAUCE (⅛ cup)

2 tbs VINEGAR (⅛ cup)

3 tsp of SUGAR

*rice, white wine, or cider vinegar... if you only have red wine vinegar, then use it!

1 small carrot

2 eggs

1 small onion or 2 spring onions

a few sprigs of mint, rinsed

2 tbs of peanuts

EQUIPMENT:

large frying pan or wok

spoon or spatula
wooden or silicone

knife & chopping board

PRE-COOK the noodles according to the packet instructions:

- some need soaking in cold water for 10 minutes
- others in boiling water
- some need actual cooking for a few minutes.

Then:
DRAIN.

Meanwhile, CUT the chicken into bite-sized pieces.

PEEL & CHOP *very finely*:

the onion

the carrot

&

the garlic.

PEEL and GRATE the ginger.

CHOP the peanuts

or CRUSH them by putting them in a small plastic bag, TYING it with a knot, then CRUSHING them with a jar...

or rolling pin.

HEAT the oil in the pan or wok. FRY the chicken, on a high heat, stirring constantly with a wooden spoon, until it starts to brown. ADD: *the garlic, onion, carrot, soy sauce, vinegar, sugar and a small glass of water.* Keep STIRRING.

high HEAT

PUSH the ingredients to the side of the pan and BREAK the eggs into the empty space. STIR, breaking the yolks, then MIX in, little by little, the noodles and other ingredients.
COOK for a further 2-3 minutes STIRRING.

STIR

Transfer

to plates, SPRINKLE with the peanuts and torn mint leaves.

pasta night

Extras

1. You can leave out the chicken or substitute with any kind of protein: cubed tofu, prawns, pieces of fish, turkey...

2. You can also add more vegetables, like fresh peas, chopped cabbage or bok choy, chopped broccoli... a good way to use any bits and pieces left in the fridge.

one pan Real Steak & blue sauce

EFFORT: ***
serves: 2 people
PREP TIME: 10 MINUTES

INGREDIENTS :

tbs = tablespoon

1 large
or 2 smaller steaks

100 g (4 oz) of blue cheese

salt & pepper

crème fraîche or double cream
150 ML (5 FL OZ / ⅔ CUP)

OIL 2 tbs (⅛ cup)

EQUIPMENT:

frying pan *or* grill pan

ALUMINIUM FOIL

spatula *or wooden spoon*

OIL and lightly **pepper** the meat.

HEAT the pan *gently*. LAY the meat in the hot pan. On a medium heat, COOK for about

2 min* on each side

*This depends on the thickness of the cut and how well you like your meat done.

ADD some **salt** and REMOVE to a plate. COVER with some foil (or an other plate) to keep warm.

WIPE the pan... *with a paper towel.*

PLACE back on a low heat. ADD cheese and cream and let everything MELT *slowly* and thicken a little.

THE CREAM

low heat

POUR over the meat.

Eat with boiled potatoes, oven baked fries, a green salad. Or just a chunk of bread.

Plan B (if you don't like blue cheese) • ADD a little **water** to the pan once the meat has been removed (even a little **wine** if you have some open). ADD some **dijon mustard** and a little **salt**. Let this BOIL on a highish heat, SCRAPING the pan with the spatula, so that it reduces a little and makes a nice « jus » (juice, or sauce) for your meat.

in need of meat

mustardy & creamy **Express Chicken**

EFFORT: *
serves: 2 people
PREP TIME: 15 MINUTES

INGREDIENTS :

tbs = tablespoon

2 chicken breasts

1-2 tbs
(⅛ cup) of dijon mustard

4 tbs
(2 fl oz/ ¼ cup) of crème fraîche

salt & pepper

2 tbs (⅛ cup) oil

EQUIPMENT:

frying pan

HEAT the oil in a frying pan, on a medium heat. PUT the chicken in the pan, laying it flat, and COOK on one side until *lightly golden*.

oil

TURN OVER

& cook the other side.

LOWER the heat. ADD the mustard and cream, MIXING everything *gently* together in the pan. LET the chicken finish cooking:

crème fraîche   mix

mustard

about 10 mins,

depending on the thickness of the meat.

To test if the chicken is cooked :

1 : PIERCE with a knife: the juices should run clear,

<u>not</u> pink.

clear juice

2 : If you are not sure, CUT right through the chicken: there should be no traces of *pink.*

Serve the chicken by POURING the sauce over it, SCRAPING the frying pan clean.

SEASON with salt & pepper and eat with bread, rice or potatoes, and maybe some salad too.

in need of meat

15

Turkey & Avocado

INGREDIENTS :

tbs = tablespoon

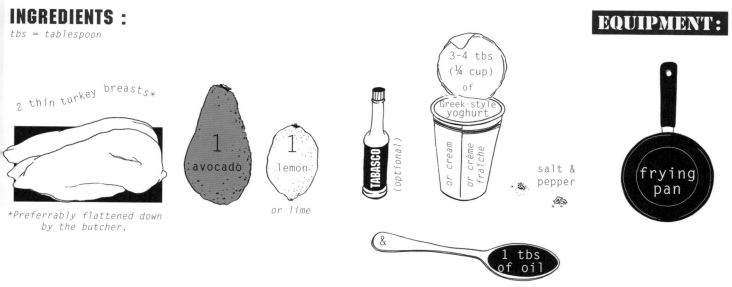

2 thin turkey breasts*

*Preferrably flattened down by the butcher.

1 avocado

1 lemon
or lime

TABASCO *(optional)*

3-4 tbs (¼ cup) of Greek-style yoghurt
or cream or crème fraîche

salt & pepper

&
1 tbs of oil

EQUIPMENT:

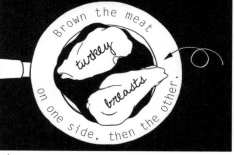

frying pan

PEEL and CUT the avocado into LARGE chunks.

It's ok if large solid pieces remain, it doesn't need to be a purée, just a little smashed.

MASH roughly with a fork, *adding lemon juice to prevent it from blackening*, and ADD:

some TABASCO

salt & pepper

HEAT the oil in a pan, on a highish heat.

Brown the meat *turkey breasts* on one side, then the other.

The turkey should cook in about 10 minutes, if the breasts are thin enough, otherwise lower the heat and leave to cook a little longer.

When it is cooked, **LOWER the heat** and ADD the mashed avocado and yoghurt, cream or crème fraîche.

Stir....

& REMOVE from the heat *quickly* (you don't want to actually cook the avocado).

Serve...

with potatoes

or rice, for example.

« not quite » Fish Fingers

EFFORT: **
serves: 2 people
PREP TIME: 30 MINUTES

oven

INGREDIENTS :

tbs = tablespoon
tsp = teaspoon

2 fish fillets
(any kind you like)

50 g
(2 oz/½ stick)
of butter

salt & pepper

1 lemon

6 tbs (½ cup) of breadcrumbs

EQUIPMENT:

oven dish

grater or zester

saucepan

& to make this more interesting:

a few sprigs of fresh herbs of your choice, rinsed, dried, chopped

1 very finely chopped spring onion or shallot

1 tsp of paprika or a pinch of cayenne pepper

zest of the lemon

a small piece of fresh ginger, peeled and grated

a dash of Tabasco or chilli sauce

Place the fish fillets in an oven dish.

PREHEAT **the oven** to **220°C** (425°F/Gas 7)

SPRINKLE with breadcrumbs. SEASON.

salt, pepper + herbs

ADD the ingredients of your choice: the chopped herbs, spices.

MELT the butter in a small saucepan. ADD:

half the *juice of the lemon*

the ginger*

the zest*

the onion*

*if you wish.

POUR ... over the fish.

COOK for 10-15 mins, depending on the thickness of the fish.

The cooked fish should flake easily with **a fork** but should still remain quite firm...

fish fix

17

Sardine Butter

EFFORT: *
serves: 2 people
PREP TIME: 10 MINUTES

no cooking

INGREDIENTS :

tbs = tablespoon

1 tin of SARDINES

some tomatoes, to serve *(optional)*

some bread

a dash of TABASCO *
*or any sauce you like

1 lemon

15 G (½ oz / 1 tbs) of butter*
*left to soften a little

EQUIPMENT:

grater or zester *(optional)*

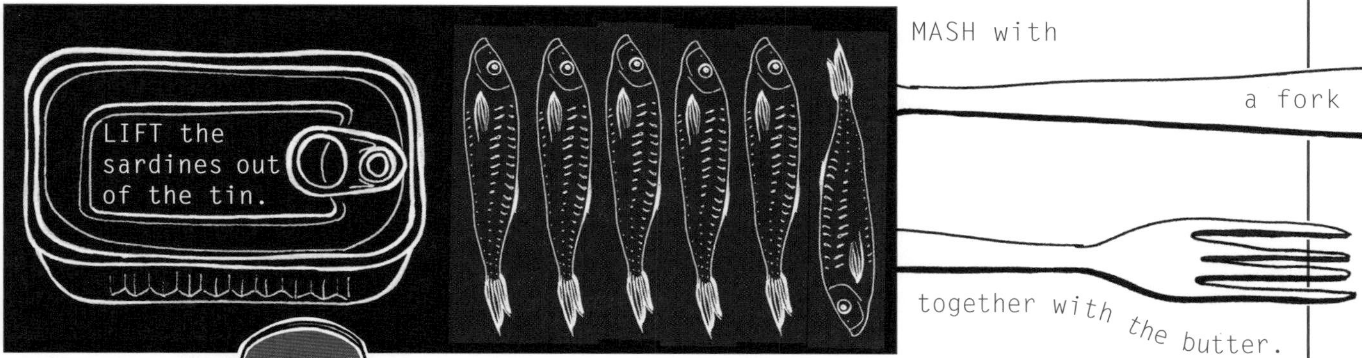

LIFT the sardines out of the tin.

MASH with a fork together with the butter.

ADD...

a dash of your favourite sauce

a little lemon juice.

& the zest *(optional)*

MIX...

Serve with some bread and tomatoes.

A QUICK SNACK

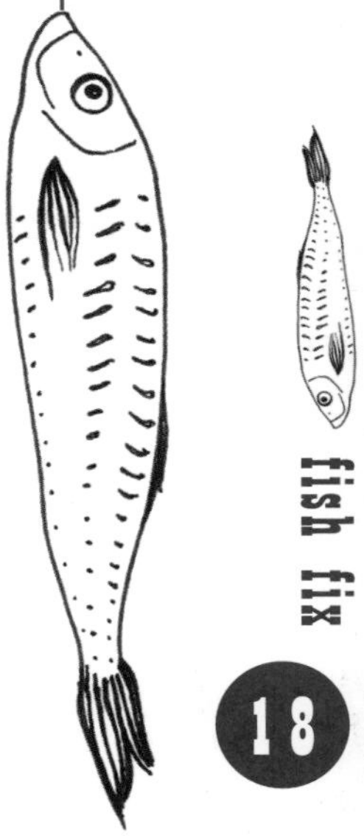

fish fix

18

Smoked Mackerel Pâté

EFFORT: *
serves: 2 people
PREP TIME: 10 MINUTES

no cooking

INGREDIENTS :

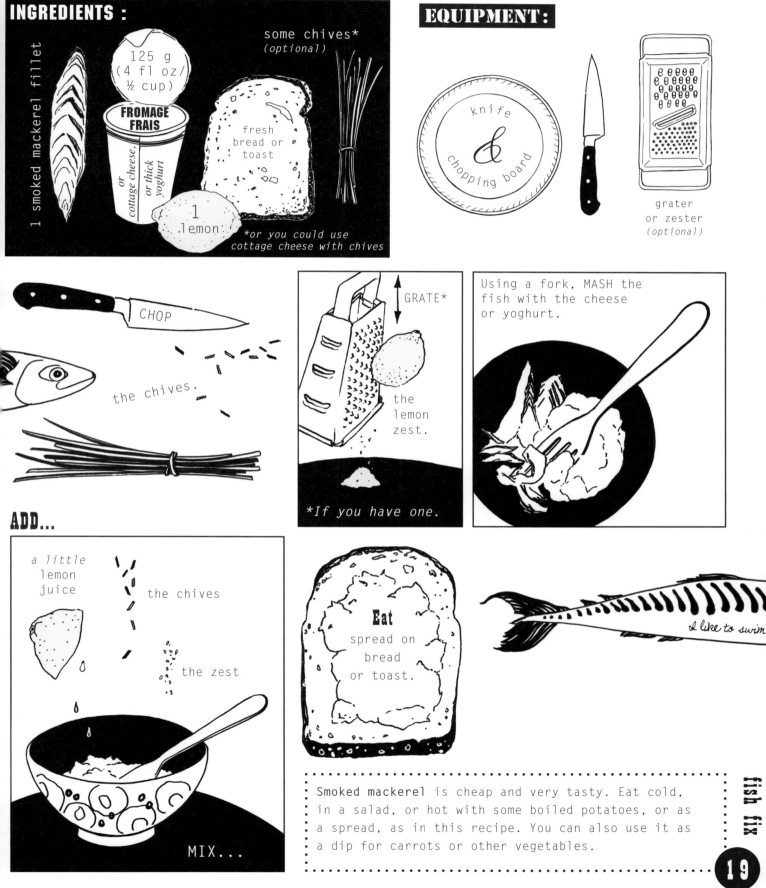

1 smoked mackerel fillet

125 g (4 fl oz/ ½ cup) FROMAGE FRAIS or cottage cheese, or thick yoghurt

1 lemon

fresh bread or toast

some chives* (optional)

*or you could use cottage cheese with chives

EQUIPMENT:

knife & chopping board

grater or zester (optional)

CHOP the chives.

GRATE* the lemon zest.

*If you have one.

Using a fork, MASH the fish with the cheese or yoghurt.

ADD...

a little lemon juice

the chives

the zest

MIX...

Eat spread on bread or toast.

I like to swim

Smoked mackerel is cheap and very tasty. Eat cold, in a salad, or hot with some boiled potatoes, or as a spread, as in this recipe. You can also use it as a dip for carrots or other vegetables.

fish fix

19

Raw Fish « Tahitian style »

EFFORT: *
serves: 2 people
PREP TIME: 45 MINUTES#

no cooking

includes 30 mins resting time

INGREDIENTS :

EQUIPMENT:

1 very fresh
fish fillet
(200 g / 7 oz)

(5 fl oz / ²/₃ cup)
of coconut milk

2-3 limes

¼ of a cucumber

1 carrot

salt & pepper

knife &
chopping board

grater

dish

DICE the fish.

REMOVE
any bones.

PLACE in a dish.
SEASON with:

some salt & pepper.

POUR over the coconut milk
and the juice of one lime.
MIX gently.

COCONUT MILK

TASTE the marinade and
ADD more juice if necessary.
Leave to REST for about
__30 minutes.__

Meanwhile, PEEL and GRATE
the carrot and cucumber
with the coarse side
of the grater.

Mix gently
with the fish.

Eat with some bread

or...

rice.

Extras This is a very basic recipe for raw fish. The fish is actually « cooked » by the lime juice,
so if you prefer the taste and texture of really raw fish, don't let it marinate for too long!
Plan B You can customise this recipe by adding some crushed garlic, a little finely grated fresh
ginger, a dash of soy sauce, a dash of spicy sauce. OR sprinkle with some sesame or poppy seeds...

fish fix

Green Fish Curry
the easiest possible

EFFORT: **
serves: 2 people
PREP TIME: 25 MINUTES

or micro wave
optional

INGREDIENTS :
tbs = tablespoon; tsp = teaspoon

1 tbs OF OIL

1 tbs of green CURRY PASTE

COCONUT MILK
300 ml (10 fl oz/ 1¼ cups)

½ cube of organic vegetable stock (or 1 tsp stock powder)

150-200 g (1-1¼ cups) FROZEN SPINACH or PEAS

400 g (14 oz) of fish fillets

RICE to serve

½ bunch of *coriander*

EQUIPMENT:

SAUCEPAN
OR
microwavable container for the rice

large frying pan*
*or LARGE saucepan or wok

wooden spoon

COOK the rice... on the stove or in the microwave.

CUT the fish into **LARGE** cubes.

HEAT the oil in a large pan. **ADD** the curry paste & **FRY**, **on a high heat,** stirring with a wooden spoon, for about 30 seconds.

l'huile   30 sec

ADD: the stock & a large glass of water.

BRING to the boil.

STIR to dissolve the stock, and **LOWER** the heat to a *gentle* simmer.

COCONUT MILK

ADD the fish and the vegetables, **COOK** for about **5** to **10** minutes, depending on the size of the pieces of fish...

taste!

RINSE the coriander, pat **DRY** with a paper towel and pick off the leaves. **SPRINKLE** onto the curry.

Serve with the rice.

You can use one type of fish or a combination.

Serve with croûtons & ice cubes...

A very simple Gazpacho-style Soup

EFFORT: *
serves: 2 people
PREP TIME: 20 MINUTES

no cooking

INGREDIENTS :

tbs = tablespoon

6 *ripe tom-a-toes*

1 red capsicum (pepper)

1 onion

1 CUCUMBER

pepper

spicy sauce

OLIVE OIL 3 tbs (¼ cup)

6 ice cubes

&

12 croûtons

+ salt

EQUIPMENT:

SAUCEPAN*

*or kettle for boiling water

hand-held mixer or blender

BOIL some water. PUT the tomatoes in a large bowl or pan

&

COVER with the boiling water.

STAND for a few minutes.

PEEL off the skin.

CUT into **CHUNKS**.

PEEL the cucumber & CUT into chunks.

REMOVE the white parts of the capsicum... & the seeds.

Then CUT into chunks.

PEEL the onion & CUT into chunks.

Put all the vegetables in the mixer or blender and PROCESS. ADD some water if necessary &...

Chill in the fridge.
Serve with croûtons and ice cubes.

the oil

some salt + pepper

some sauce

• This is the simplest possible recipe for a gazpacho-style summer soup. It is also nice to add bits of stale bread, or chopped herbs (some mint maybe) or even some summer fruit: chunks of melon, watermelon or ripe peach give an interesting twist.
• You could also save some whole bits of vegetable, cut them into tiny dice and lay them on top of the soup just before serving.

veggie forever

22

Red Lentil Soup
all-in-one

EFFORT: *
serves: 2 people
PREP TIME: 30 MINUTES#

#(including 20 mins cooking)

or micro wave

INGREDIENTS :

tsp = teaspoon

200 G (7 OZ / ¾ CUP) OF **RED LENTILS***

*(available in most supermarkets, health food or Indian shops)

a tin of TOMATOES

1 onion

1 clove of garlic

2 tsp of spice (garam masala or curry powder, or ras el hanout)

CURRY 2 tsp

100 ml (3 fl oz/½ cup) coconut milk (or Greek-style yoghurt)

COCONUT

1 lemon **OR** lime

pepper
salt

EQUIPMENT:

LARGE saucepan

OR

large microwave container

hand-held mixer, blender or processor

sieve

RINSE the lentils in a sieve.

PEEL and CUT the onion and garlic into large **CHUNKS**...

(or more *finely* if you don't have a blender or mixer).

PLACE all the ingredients in a large saucepan (except the lime and coconut milk or yoghurt).

ADD 3 large glasses of water

BRING to a *gentle boil*

Cook for about 20 minutes. **The lentils will break down.**

---

blend the soup

if you don't have one, it will be fine as it is.

ADD:

most of the coconut *milk** *or yoghurt

a little lime or lemon juice

pepper
salt

VERY LOW HEAT

ADD...

the rest of the coconut milk or yoghurt

SERVE.

You can make this soup in the microwave by putting all the ingredients (except the coconut milk and lemon) in a container and cooking on medium power for about 10 minutes (depending on your microwave).

veggie forever

23

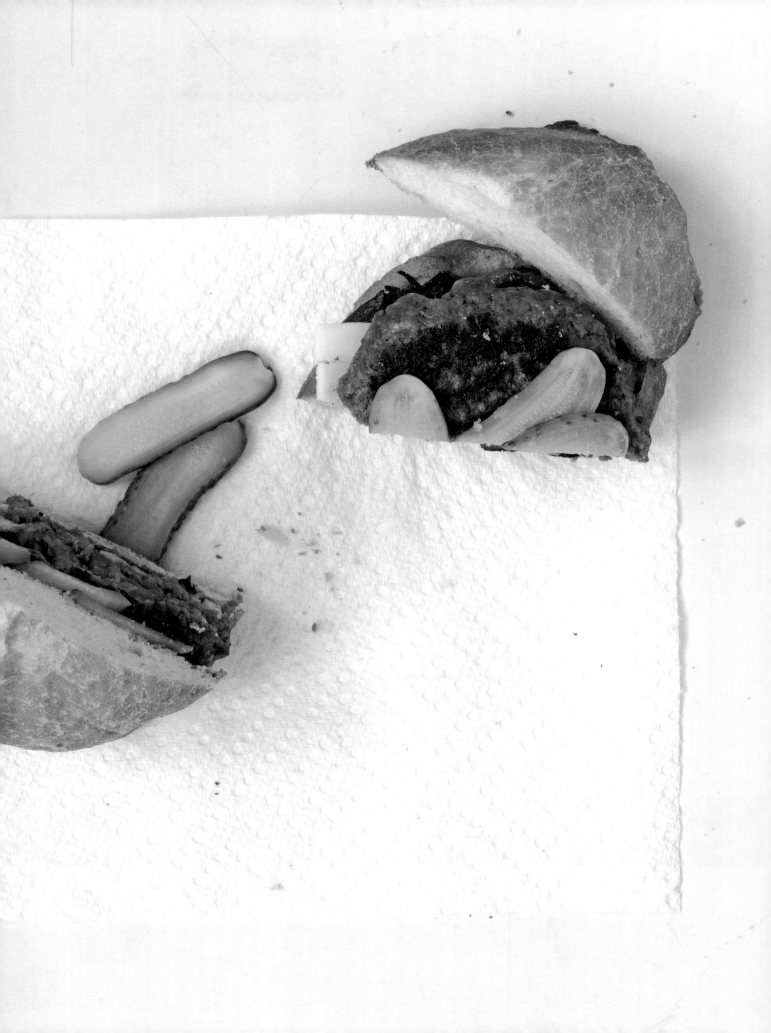

Homemade Burger

EFFORT: **
serves: 2 people
PREP TIME: 15 MINUTES

grill & *or toaster*

INGREDIENTS :

tbs = tablespoon

2 burger buns

salt + pepper

1 tbs OIL

SOME KETCHUP

SAUCE

a dash of worcestershire sauce (or chilli sauce, brown sauce, hp sauce, bbq sauce...)

350-400 g (12-14 oz) of BEEF MINCE

or 2 nice steaks or 2 pieces of beef fillet

2 slices of aged cheddar cheese

PICKLED GHERKINS

1 small onion or 1 tbs of onion jam

EQUIPMENT:

+ a choice of:

4-6 slices of cooked beetroot

OR 1 ripe avocado

OR 150 g (5 oz) of blue cheese

frying pan

TOAST the buns.

SLICE the onion thinly.

BEEF MINCE:

COMBINE the mince with the sauce and SEASON with salt and pepper....

MIX

SHAPE into burgers.

COOK in a frying pan, on a medium to high heat, with a little oil.

STEAKS:

Or COOK the steaks in the oil...

...**then** SEASON with salt, pepper and the sauce.

SAUCE

MAKE UP the burgers:

half a bun

the extras : avocado or beetroot or blue cheese

more sauce ? *more cheese ?*

the meat

the cheese slices

the onion slices or onion jam

a little ketchup sliced pickled gherkins

half a bun

not so junk

Homestyle Club Sandwich

EFFORT: **
serves: 2 people
PREP TIME: 15 MINUTES

INGREDIENTS :

tsp = teaspoon

4 slices of bread

an avocado ½

2 tsp of vinegar

2 slices of bacon or cooked ham

2 eggs

salad sprouts (alfalfa, cress or similar, *optional*)

a little worcestershire sauce or Tabasco

some cream cheese with or without chives*

2-4 salad leaves

*or some hummus, tzatziki etc

EQUIPMENT:

frying pan *(optional)*

knife

small SAUCEPAN

6 mins

PUT the eggs in a pan of water. BRING to the boil and cook for 6 mins *on a gentle boil.*

← cold water

PEEL

CUT in 2

PLACE under cold running water and SHELL. CUT the eggs in half.

vinegar

PEEL the avocado and CUT into slices, SPRINKLE over a little vinegar.

medium HEAT

COOK the bacon, if using, in a small frying pan.

Press

SPREAD some cream cheese (or hummus, tzatziki, etc) onto a slice of the bread. LAY the slices of avocado on top, then PRESS *lightly* with a knife.

SPRINKLE over a little sauce, then PUT the bacon or ham on. PLACE the eggs on top of the bacon or ham.

the eggs

the bacon

ADD the salad leaves and sprouts (they give some crunch and, depending on the variety, a little heat too).

Finish with a second slice of bread (with more spread, if you like)

&...

eat.

not so junk

25

Easy Hummus

INGREDIENTS :

tbs = tablespoon
tsp = teaspoon

1 tin of chick-peas

1 lemon

2-3 tbs (¼ cup) of olive oil

1 tbs of PEANUT BUTTER (optional)

1 small clove of garlic

pepper   salt

1 tbs of shredded coconut (optional)

...and a few sprigs of coriander or mint (optional)

EQUIPMENT:

LARGE bowl

lemon juicer

sieve

& knife board

potato masher or a fork

grater or zester

DRAIN the chickpeas ...

reserving some of the liquid.

NOTE: MAKE sure to grate only the yellow skin, not the thick bitter white skin.

GRATE ½ tsp of lemon zest.

CUT the lemon in 2 and squeeze the juice.

PEEL the garlic and CRUSH the clove with the flat side of a knife.

CRUSH

CHOP very *finely*.

MASH

ADD the peanut butter if you have it.

salt & pepper

MASH the chickpeas with 2 tbs of the oil, the lemon zest, the garlic & about 1 tsp of lemon juice.

ADD a little of the tinned chickpeas liquid if the mixture seems a bit dry.

THE texture of your mixture won't be as smooth as in usual hummus, but that's what makes it interesting!

TRANSFER to a small bowl,

& SPRINKLE with the chopped herbs

... or some toasted shredded coconut.*

*Throw coconut into an ungreased hot frying pan and stir for barely a minute until lightly browned. Take off the heat immediately as it burns very quickly.

stir!

medium heat

Serve with grissini and raw vegetable sticks...

Or use as a spread on bagels or in a sandwich, with a little grated carrot and some leftover chicken.

loadsa friends

26

Super Salsa for nachos

EFFORT: **
serves: 6 people##
PREP TIME: 15 MINUTES

no cooking

you can multiply the quantities if you have more guests

INGREDIENTS :

6 ripe tom -a- toes

1 small onion or 2 spring onions

1 small red chilli* *or some Tabasco

1 lime

PEPPER & salt

a shot of tequila or vodka

half a bunch of coriander (optional)

Alternatively: a small bunch of grapes OR ¼ of a ripe mango

EQUIPMENT:

& knife board

DICE the tomatoes as small as possible.

REMOVE the seeds from the chilli & chop into tiny pieces.

PEEL the onion and chop very finely.

RINSE, DRY & CHOP the coriander.

CHOP the fruit, if using, into small pieces.

MIX together all of the ingredients, using only a small amount of chilli & a little lime juice...

... THEN add more if necessary.

Sexy Porridge

EFFORT: *
serves: 2 people
PREP TIME: 10 MINUTES

or micro **wave**

INGREDIENTS :

tbs = tablespoon

medjool dates = a variety of dates, bigger, fatter, darker and better than the normal ones... they can be found easily in most supermarkets or delis...

2–4 medjool dates

400 ml
(14 fl oz/ 1²⁄₃ cups)
of *milk*

rolled oats

80–100 g (3–4 oz.)

*or some jam

SOME HONEY *

OR some sugar

a pinch of salt

2 tbs of cream*

OR

optional Greek-style Yoghurt

OR a knob of butter*

EQUIPMENT:

SAUCEPAN

OR

microwavable container

with a lid

knife

MICROWAVE:

PUT the oats in a microwavable container with a lid.

ADD the milk & 100 ml (½ cup) of water

the salt

the dates*

COOK on medium power for about 1½ to 2 min.

STIR

COOK AGAIN on medium power for a further 1 min. **OR**

STOVE:

PUT the oats in a saucepan.
ADD:

the milk & water*

the salt

the dates*

*100 ml (½ cup)

BRING to the boil then reduce the heat, STIR and cook...

...until the porridge reaches a **thick** consistency.

STIR from time to time

on a *low* heat

Then... whatever the method used, ADD the honey, jam or sugar and the cream, yoghurt or butter

& eat.

*To prepare the dates: cut them lengthwise, & remove the stones.

good start

DELICIOUS WITH >>> some blueberries or raspberries, fresh or frozen, instead of dates. Or with some maple syrup instead of the honey!

3 Smoothies

Banana Strawberry Lassi

INGREDIENTS :

1 banana

2 pots of natural yoghurt

1 lemon
or lime

1 punnet (250 g / 8 oz) of strawberries

EQUIPMENT :

blender

knife

RINSE & HULL the strawberries.

CUT them into pieces.

PEEL the banana & SLICE.

BLEND with the yoghurt & a little lemon or lime juice.

Mango Dream

INGREDIENTS :

2 ripe mangoes *

*(or frozen mangoes)

1 lime

1 LARGE glass of milk *

*(try soy, or almond milk for a change)

EQUIPMENT :

blender

knife

grater or zester

Finely GRATE, a little lime zest.

PEEL the fruit

& BLEND with the milk & the zest.

Middle Eastern

INGREDIENTS :

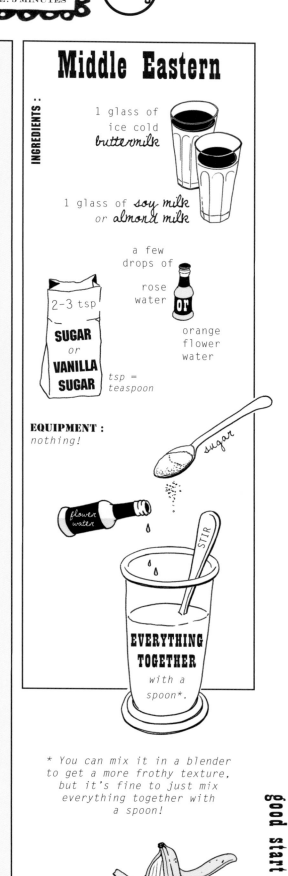

1 glass of ice cold buttermilk

1 glass of soy milk or almond milk

a few drops of rose water OR orange flower water

2-3 tsp SUGAR or VANILLA SUGAR

tsp = teaspoon

EQUIPMENT :
nothing!

STIR

EVERYTHING TOGETHER with a spoon*.

* You can mix it in a blender to get a more frothy texture, but it's fine to just mix everything together with a spoon!

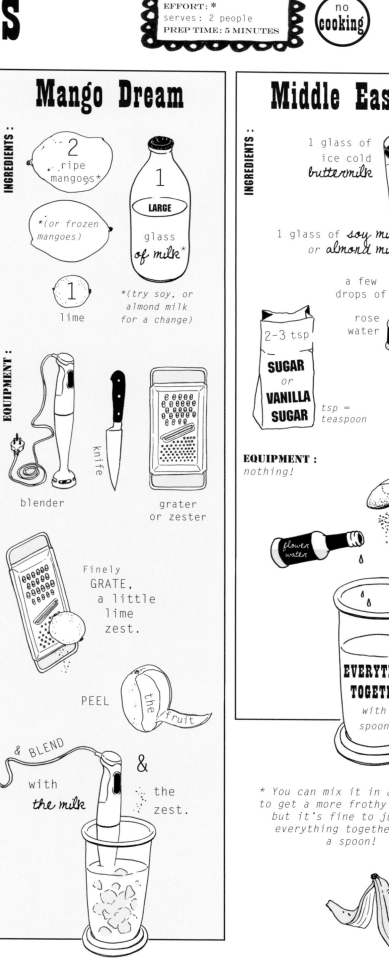

Bread & Butter Pudding

EFFORT: **
serves: 2 people
PREP TIME: 50# or 25## MIN

micro **wave** or oven

in the oven: 35 mins cooking time
in the microwave: 10 mins cooking time

INGREDIENTS :

tbs = tablespoon

6 slices of stale bread

40 g (1½ oz/ ⅓ stick) of butter

some JAM or marmalade (optional)

4-5 tbs (¼ cup) of **SUGAR**

350 ml (12 fl oz/ 1½ cups) of milk or a mix of milk and cream

EQUIPMENT:

oven dish

or

microwavable container

3 tbs of sultanas (optional) + a little **RUM** or orange juice

3 eggs

1 lemon (optional)

grater or zester

PREHEAT the oven to 180°C (350°F/Gas 4).

PUT the sultanas in the juice or rum.

BUTTER the dish or microwave container.

butter

BUTTER the bread & SPREAD with the jam.

CUT each slice in half.

CUT diagonally

*the tips of the bread should ideally stick out.

ARRANGE the slices in the dish or container, so that they point up a little.

BEAT together*

the milk (and/or cream) + the eggs + 2-3 tbs of sugar.

*with a whisk or fork.

GRATE the lemon zest. ADD the zest and the soaked sultanas. POUR over the bread*.

SPRINKLE the top with the remaining sugar.

COOK **in the oven** for about 35 minutes. It should be set and golden on top.
COOK **in the microwave** on medium power for about 5 minutes, then LET STAND inside the microwave for another 5 minutes. The pudding should be set, but will not brown like in a conventional oven.

What a mess!

INGREDIENTS :

tbs = tablespoon
tsp = teaspoon

1 LARGE meringue *
*shop bought

250 G (8 oz)
1 tub of *low fat cream cheese*

6 tbs of crème fraîche *or* mascarpone

1 punnet (250 g/8 oz) of fresh berries:
raspberries, blueberries, blackberries,
strawberries, red currants etc, or a combination

EQUIPMENT:

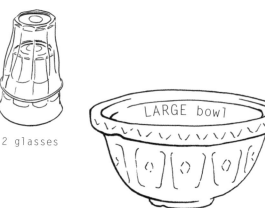

2 glasses

LARGE bowl

fork

BREAK *the meringue*

into **LARGE** pieces.

PREPARE the fruit:

RINSE* *if necessary

HULL & REMOVE any stems.

remove

PUT all the ingredients into a bowl

& STIR, *very gently**

*you don't need to blend it, you merely want to combine the ingredients and crush the berries lightly so that their juice starts to mix with everything else.

TRANSFER into **2** glasses.

PUT into the fridge for a while or **eat** *immediately.*

Instant Chocolate Mousse

EFFORT: *   serves: 2 people   PREP TIME : 5 MINUTES

COMBINE **2** pots of Greek-style yoghurt with

1 tbs of cocoa powder
(if unsweetened, add 2 tsp of sugar)

& STIR *vigorously...*

sweet tooth

31

Pretend Trifle

EFFORT: **
serves: 2 people
PREP TIME: 20 MINUTES

no cooking

INGREDIENTS :

tbs = tablespoon

2 oranges

some cognac, sweet wine or a dash of Grand Marnier...

2 thick slices of shop-bought madeira or butter cake

2 tbs of SUGAR *

or more if you like it sweet

150 ml (5 fl oz/ ²/₃ cup) of single cream

&

100 g (4 oz) of Greek-style yoghurt

1 punnet of strawberries (250 g/8 oz)

1 banana

EQUIPMENT:

2 bowls

large bowl for mixing

whisk

PUT a piece of cake into each of the two bowls.

alcohol + juice

x2

POUR over... ...the alcohol and the juice from the oranges.

RINSE and HULL the strawberries,

keeping aside 2 nice ones to decorate.

1

2

CUT the rest into pieces,

& PUT on top of the cake.

PEEL and SLICE the banana, and ADD to the strawberries.

In another bowl, WHIP the cream until it forms soft peaks*.

ADD the sugar & the yoghurt.

Put into the bowls. DECORATE with the saved strawberries.

Single cream whips up better when it is very cold. If necessary, put it in the freezer for a short while beforehand (but don't forget it!).

sweet tooth

Citus Salad

EFFORT: *
serves: 2 people
PREP TIME: 15 MINUTES

no cooking

INGREDIENTS :

1 grapefruit

2 oranges

4 man- -da- -rins

a small piece of crystallised (candied) ginger *(optional)*

EQUIPMENT:

knife & board

large bowl

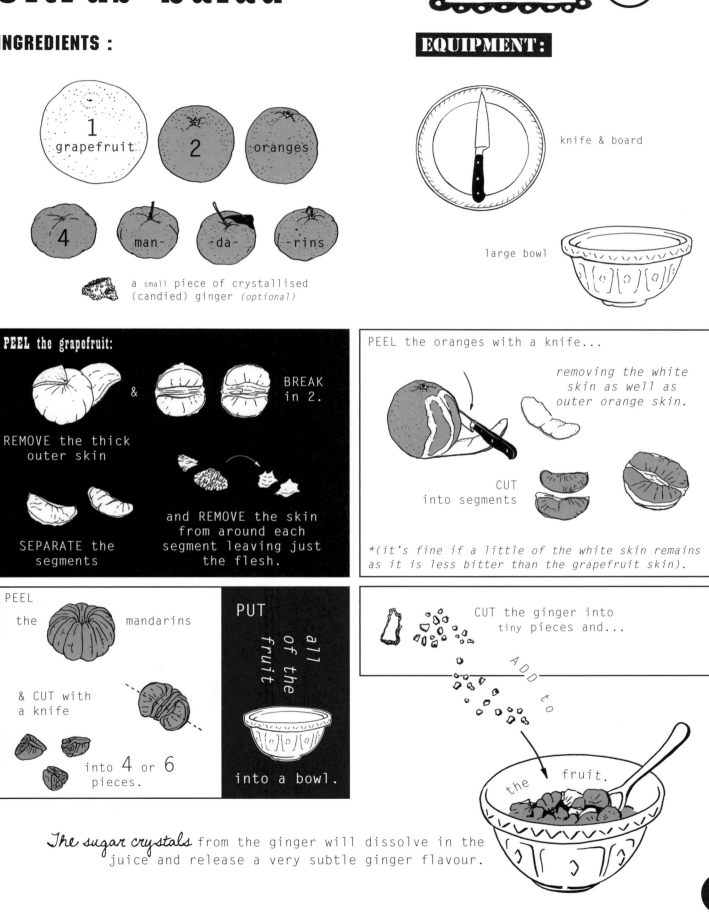

PEEL the grapefruit:

& **BREAK in 2.**

REMOVE the thick outer skin

SEPARATE the segments

and **REMOVE the skin from around each segment leaving just the flesh.**

PEEL the oranges with a knife...

removing the white skin as well as outer orange skin.

CUT into segments

(it's fine if a little of the white skin remains as it is less bitter than the grapefruit skin).

PEEL the mandarins

& **CUT with a knife**

into 4 or 6 pieces.

PUT all of the fruit into a bowl.

CUT the ginger into tiny pieces and...

ADD to the fruit.

The sugar crystals from the ginger will dissolve in the juice and release a very subtle ginger flavour.

nice 'n' fruity

33

Wake-up Strawberries
" 4 ways "

EFFORT: **
serves : 2 people
PREP TIME: 15 MINUTES#

no cooking *or*

+ *ideally 30 mins rest time*

INGREDIENTS :

tbs = tablespoon; tsp = teaspoon

1 **large** punnet of strawberries

500 g   **(16 oz)**

method 1

a glass
or
of rosé or light red wine

+

1 tbs of **SUGAR**

or

method 2

1 lemon
or lime

+

2 tbs of **SUGAR**

+

a sprig of fresh basil*

*rinsed

or method 3

of balsamic vinegar **1 tbs**

+

1 tbs of **SUGAR**

+

vanilla ICE CREAM

or

method 4

200 ml
(6 fl oz/¾ cup) of double cream

+

1 tbs of **SUGAR**

+

a glass of guava or mango *nectar*

EQUIPMENT:

knife

LARGE bowl

saucepan **(method 2)**

large bowl & whisk **(method 4)**

RINSE & HULL the strawberries.

CUT into: **2**   **4** OR **6** *pieces, depending on their size.*

---

method 1 :

PUT them into a **LARGE** bowl.

ADD:

the wine & *the sugar*

MIX *very gently* & *ideally,* LET STAND for **30** mins.

or method 2 :

PUT:
the basil leaves
the sugar
a glass of water
into a small saucepan

BRING to the boil, stirring. SIMMER for 5 mins.

REMOVE the basil leaves, & ADD *a little* the lemon or lime juice.

Let it cool **&** *pour over the strawberries.*

or method 3 :

STIR together the vinegar and sugar.

ADD to the strawberries & MIX gently.

LEAVE to MARINATE for about **30 mins.**

Serve with *vanilla icecream.*

or method 4 :

POUR the cream into a large bowl and WHISK until it forms soft peaks.

whisk

ADD 2 *tsp* of **SUGAR.**

POUR the *fruit nectar* over the strawberries, ADD a little sugar and...

SERVE with the cream.

nice 'n' fruity

34

Keda Black, the author:

Thank you to my two editors, Catie from London and Rosemarie à Paris.
And thank you Alice: beautiful work!

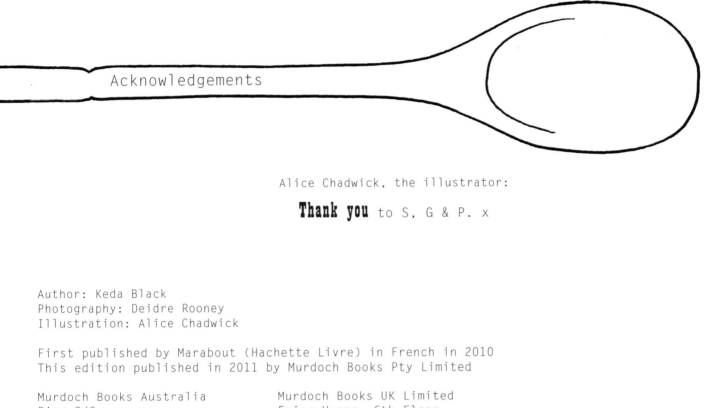

Acknowledgements

Alice Chadwick, the illustrator:

Thank you to S, G & P. x

Author: Keda Black
Photography: Deidre Rooney
Illustration: Alice Chadwick

First published by Marabout (Hachette Livre) in French in 2010
This edition published in 2011 by Murdoch Books Pty Limited

Murdoch Books Australia
Pier 8/9
23 Hickson Road
Millers Point NSW 2000
Phone: +61 (0) 2 8220 2000
Fax: +61 (0) 2 8220 2558
www.murdochbooks.com.au

Murdoch Books UK Limited
Erico House, 6th Floor
93-99 Upper Richmond Road
Putney, London SW15 2TG
Phone: +44 (0) 20 8785 5995
Fax: +44 (0) 20 8785 5985
www.murdochbooks.co.uk

Copyright © Hachette Livre — Marabout 2010

National Library of Australia Cataloguing-in-Publication entry
Author: Black, Keda.
Title: The illustrated student cookbook : a step-by-step guide to everyday
               essentials/ Keda Black.
ISBN: 978-174266-341-8 (hbk.)
Subjects: Low budget cooking.
Dewey Number: 641.552

A catalogue record for this book is available from the British Library.

Printed by Hang Tai Printing Company Limited.

+ Survival Kit +

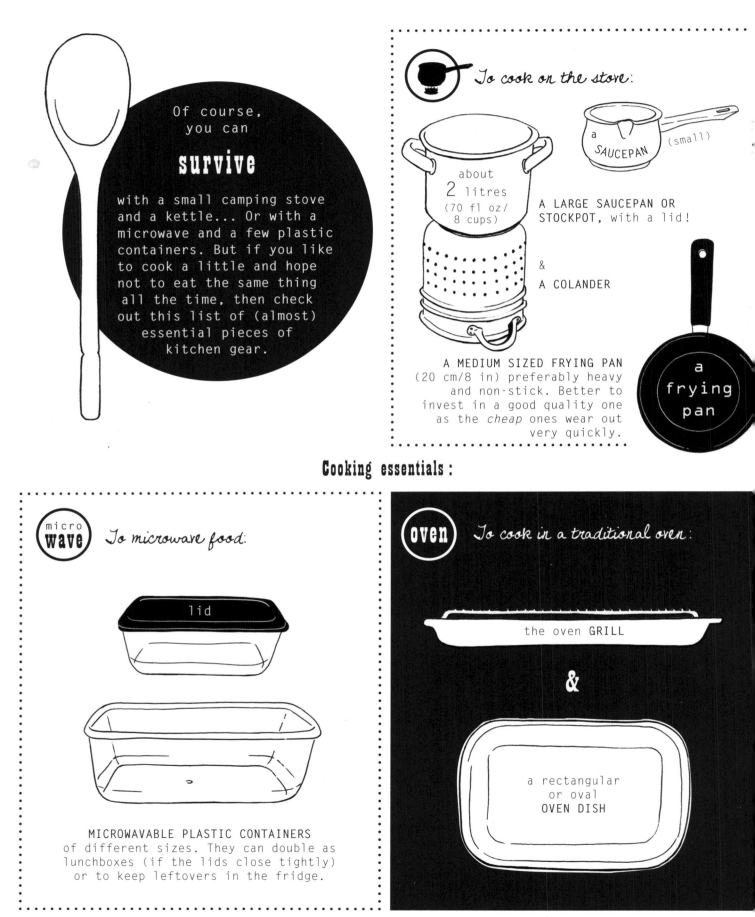

Of course, you can **survive** with a small camping stove and a kettle... Or with a microwave and a few plastic containers. But if you like to cook a little and hope not to eat the same thing all the time, then check out this list of (almost) essential pieces of kitchen gear.

To cook on the stove:

about **2** litres (70 fl oz/ 8 cups)

a SAUCEPAN (small)

A LARGE SAUCEPAN OR STOCKPOT, with a lid!

&

A COLANDER

A MEDIUM SIZED FRYING PAN (20 cm/8 in) preferably heavy and non-stick. Better to invest in a good quality one as the *cheap* ones wear out very quickly.

a frying pan

Cooking essentials :

micro wave — To microwave food:

lid

MICROWAVABLE PLASTIC CONTAINERS of different sizes. They can double as lunchboxes (if the lids close tightly) or to keep leftovers in the fridge.

oven — To cook in a traditional oven:

the oven GRILL

&

a rectangular or oval OVEN DISH